**NEA
EARLY CHILDHOOD
EDUCATION SERIES**

Joy in Learning: Making It Happen in Early Childhood Classes

Leon H. Burton

**A NATIONAL EDUCATION ASSOCIATION
PUBLICATION**

Printing History
    First Printing: September 1991

Note

The opinions expressed in this publication should not be construed as representing the policy or position of the National Education Association. Materials published by the NEA Professional Library are intended to be discussion documents for educators who are concerned with specialized interests of the profession.

Library of Congress Cataloging-in-Publication Data

Burton, Leon.
    Joy in learning : making it happen in early childhood classes /
Leon H. Burton.
        p.   cm. — (NEA Early childhood education series)
    Includes bibliographical references.
    ISBN 0–8106–0359–4
    1. Early childhood education—United States.   I. Title.
II. Series: Early childhood education series (Washington, D.C.)
LB1139.25.B87   1991
372.21—dc20   91–3908
                                                                    CIP

CONTENTS

The Author

Leon H. Burton is Professor of Education and Project Director, Curriculum Research and Development Group, College of Education, University of Hawaii, Honolulu

The Advisory Panel

Marjean Brody, Elementary School Counselor, Fairbanks North Star Borough School District, Alaska

Jean I. Caudle, Professor, University of Wisconsin-Oshkosh; and Faculty Advisor, Student Wisconsin Education Association

Rebecca Landers, Special Education Teacher, Haleyville Elementary School, Alabama

Phyllis J. Lewis, Elementary Teacher, Jennings Elementary School, Quincy, Michigan

Evelyn Metoyer Williams, Early Childhood Education Teacher, Richland Avenue Children's Center, Los Angeles

PREFACE

Their lips become thin as a smile gradually begins to form and spread across the face. The dancing sparkles in their eyes clearly indicate that something exciting, compelling, and enjoyable is beginning to happen. Little tilts of the head, subtle movements of body parts, a general "fidget" state all become part of a physical orchestration that acknowledges the arrival of a new experience and understanding. Then a beaming face and other childlike qualities combine to show satisfaction and joy as learning takes place. Yes, it is a wonderful experience to observe early childhood teachers learn new content and develop new skills that will equip them to do their job better. What an exciting group of learners are the teachers of young children! There is little difference in the way they and young children learn, but enjoyment is truly a key to success at any educational level.

This monograph has been prepared for teachers of young children, one of the most enjoyable groups of learners that I have experienced during my career as an educator. The joy I derived in working with teachers at this level has inspired me to take a close look at the *joy* theme in an attempt to learn more about what causes feelings of joy and pleasure during the teaching and learning process. This inspiration has led to the conclusion that *all* learning at any level should be challenging, interesting, and enjoyable. It is my intent in this monograph to provide or suggest additional insights that will be useful to teachers in helping them to become even more successful in presenting joy-filled learning programs to young children.

Chapter 1

A PHILOSOPHY
FOR EARLY EDUCATION

THE NATURE OF YOUNG CHILDREN

Young children everywhere are filled with curiosity. As soon as they learn to crawl, their instincts lead them to embark upon explorations to manipulate, inspect, enjoy, experience at a close range to touch, grasp, taste, feel, smell, shake, pull and to establish a physical relationship with most things in their immediate environment. Curiosity and an inquiring mind develop in a natural way in the very early years. Hence, the stimulation of originality, imagination, spontaneity, independence, openness, intuition, inquiry, and exploration is essential to the continued development of the child's inherent potential. These early years are a time for children *to learn how to learn* and to build an inner excitement for continued learning and greater explorations.

Young children are social beings. They have an inherent urge to interact with and react to the people in their environment. It is from these interactive experiences that they begin to discover meanings in "people actions", learning about such things as values, order, procedures, standards, rules, courtesies, and other matters that contribute to their socialization. To be with other people, to be given personal attention and approval by adults is a high-priority need of the young child. It is primarily from their experiences with adult models that children develop acceptable social skills and learn to intellectualize about their relationships with others.

Because young children are social beings filled with curiosity, the major foci for early education programs seem

9

apparent. The curiosity-filled and social-seeking child should be guided by organized schooling to build upon these inherent instincts. Moreover, these instincts should form a base from which children are provided with the contexts for new and enjoyable adventures that will broaden their interests and open new areas of experience that may not be a part of their immediate environment.

As their motor development becomes further refined, and their intellectual-social development is expanded, children should be introduced to subject matter that has direct relatedness to their accumulated experiences. A primary concern of organized learning, then, is the design of learning contexts that are based on children's natural forms of learning, but that gradually go beyond them to open up new and related adventures, explorations, and creative opportunities at levels where success can be anticipated.

LEARNING CONTEXTS

Traditionally, learning contexts for schools are drawn from such subjects as language arts, social studies, health/science/technology, art, music, physical education, and mathematics. Because these subjects have a universal appeal—and they especially have application potential in out adult world—it therefore seems appropriate to draw content from them to design programs for all levels of education, particularly for childhood education.

In childhood education, however, the contexts should correspond with the natural growth (capacity and experience) of children and employ corresponding modes of presentation. Facts, principles, laws, technical skills, conceptual taxonomies, and an expanding general information base are often the staple of higher curricular areas, but the topics drawn from the subjects to create learning contexts for childhood education should have life relevancy and become a part of the child's actual experience. Given these characteristics, the contexts for younger children should: (1) be concrete and utilitarian in nature, gradually becoming more abstract; (2) meet the personal needs of children, gradually becoming more focused on the needs for successful participation in society; and (3) have a performance orientation, gradually requiring greater intellectualization; and (4) these learning contexts should establish vital connective understandings and threads of continuity between experiences at lower and higher levels.

Young minds develop best in a warm, inviting and social environment. Learning contexts will therefore be more effective when topics from the subjects are approached through play, games, conversation, pictorial imagination, stories, shared reflections on life events and family activities, songs, and personal and group involvement in social tasks. Heavy use of drill-type activities and exercises and worksheet tasks will not provide the kind of active, manipulative, and creative environment essential to the development of young minds.

SOCIETAL EXPECTATIONS

Society rightly expects positive results from schooling; hence, the foundation for social, physical, and intellectual development laid in the early years becomes vital to the success of schooling at higher levels and to adult life. Preparation for effective participation in society should include developmentally appropriate contexts for children to learn to assume such diverse roles as economist, naturalist, nurse, administrator, artist, teacher, communicator, businessperson, agriculturalist, and so on. Assuming such roles in a childhood education program is an active process that will have lifelong practical applications. The process will also establish relevance between study in the subject areas and participation in real-world activities. A program

11

consisting of the right kinds of learning contexts will equip children to begin interesting and enjoyable journeys that can lead to effective and fulfilling life membership in society.

Chapter 2

CHILD DEVELOPMENT

The successful early childhood teacher is a facilitator and exemplar of child development principles, and as a successful guide to joy in learning, he/she must have a background in child development theories. It is crucial to the lives of young children that a positive foundation for learning be laid in the early years, from which mature development can proceed. Teacher knowledge of *how* children learn is directly related to both successful and enjoyable learning. Gaining an in-depth understanding of learning theories as well as observing children learning, consulting with colleagues to learn their personal theories of successful and enjoyable learning, becoming familiar with research studies, and discussing with children their perceptions of how they learn are all helpful avenues to building a reservoir of thought about the ways that children learn.

It is important to the successful planning and delivery of educational activities to become knowledgeable about children's age/developmental levels and capabilities. Information regarding both generalized sets of capabilities and capabilities related to specific subject areas is available to teachers for review and use. Those who fail to develop a good acquaintance with such information lists will have a *missing link* in their attempts to understand the educational experiences of children. Exceptions to developmental levels and capabilities lists will always be found, but such lists do provide valuable clues and guidelines for planning educational activity

The following are some of the important areas of child development that relate to changes in society and the perceived needs of all children:

1. Independence
2. Self-esteem
3. Cooperative interaction
4. Creative expression
5. Problem solving
6. Physical capability

These six areas seem to subsume many other areas and are described in detail below. Other areas to be aware of are responsibility, decision making, self-motivation, respect, loving and caring, sense of time, sense of space, order and sequence, and values of learning.

INDEPENDENCE

Young children need to gradually be given the freedom to make choices and to feel a sense of control of their environment. This kind of freedom leads both to a general awareness of responsibility and to a recognition of the need to accept responsibility for one's actions. The freedom to think independently is essential to developing both a will and a desire to accept responsibility. Hence, the stimulation of curiosity, inquisitiveness, exploration, and discovery are important to the development of independence. As their understanding of independence expands, young children will learn to anticipate the outcome of their actions even before they act, and they will establish boundaries of respect for successful interaction with others. Independent learning is a goal to strive for in guiding the development of young children because ultimately it will lead to lifelong joy in learning.

SELF-ESTEEM

It is of extreme importance that young children be given opportunities to be successful in their eductional activities and to develop a sense of pride in their accomplishments. The level of self-esteem children have will influence their success in all of their life activities. Self-esteem has vital connections with other areas of child development such as positive self-concept, independence, self-motivation, loving and caring, self-evaluation, and valuing learning. Therefore, it is important in the formative years for children to see their work displayed and to be given praise for their efforts (when praise is warranted). The realization of a sense of achievement resulting from the development of self-esteem is linked to the degree of joy children will find in learning and in all of life.

COOPERATIVE INTERACTION

The cooperative interaction skills young children develop also relate to the degree of joy they will experience in learning. Social interaction is a vital element of learning in school, and those who learn to interact successfully experience more success and joy in their school life. Young children often will develop a sense of their own identity while they participate in group activity and gradually develop an understanding of their individual obligation to group success. Developing tolerance for the views of others, learning to view group work as a noncompetitive activity, forming friendships, learning to listen to others, and working toward group consensus helps to build both individual and group identification. Of special importance are the processes of cooperative interaction forged through play, a much more intense learning mode in which children relate to others. A sense of belonging in group activity encourages the building of trust in others and sets the stage for enjoyable relationships and learning activities.

CREATIVE EXPRESSION

Young children learn to express themselves creatively when they have the freedom to invent, experiment, explore, originate, follow instincts, and examine. At times they may even get off the main track of learning, taking steps into the unknown to satisfy their curiosity and pursue original ideas. Learning to think and express oneself creatively often requires deviation from a traditional educational mold. Young children will find great joy in having occasions to contribute original ideas, share differing views, and find new ways to look at problems. Too many rigidly organized tasks, an overemphasis on memorization, strict control that limits questioning, conditions that result in children becoming fearful of a new approach, and other such educational settings can block the development of creative expression. Joyful learning will be realized only to the degree that creative thought and expression is an integral part of the total educational program for young children.

PROBLEM SOLVING

Problem-solving activities are valuable to children's overall intellectual development and to their abilities to *learn how to learn.* Such activities usually are teacher initiated, and teacher presentations should stimulate children's curiosity, leading them to the discovery of solutions. Both structured procedures and unstructured experimentations without explicit procedures for finding solutions can provide children with opportunities to learn new information and develop increasingly complex problem-solving skills. It is through problem-solving opportunities that children even can experience self-discovery. The stimulation of divergent thinking is especially valuable since it can lead to several correct answers to a given problem. Problem-solving skills are the lifeblood of higher levels of maturity and they contribute directly to the degree of joy children will experience in educational activity.

PHYSICAL CAPABILITY

Regular exercise of a growing body and the development of coordination, balance, endurance, and strength are central to

16

young children in becoming functional physically and in finding joy in life. Gross and fine motor skill development are important components of children's early learning experiences. The ancient Greek ideal "a sound mind in a sound body" certainly has value for early childhood education today. A variety of activities should be provided to children for the development of hand and eye coordination, manual dexterity, coordination of movement with sound stimuli, playground skills (e.g., climbing, chasing, tagging, pulling, pushing, pedaling), and for a general burning and release of pent-up energy—vital functions for both the physical and mental health of young children. The feeling of wellness is a major contributor to joy in the life of a child.

Chapter 3

JOY AND PLEASURE

Joy is an interesting concept to consider for those who elect to plumb its deeper meanings in relation to schooling and learning. In a general way, joy is the pleasure, satisfaction, and glad feelings one derives from a sense of well-being. Joy has been described as an altered or enhanced sense of self that changes the way we view the world and the way we are viewed by others. People of all ages need the assurance of well-being in life—in school, in the home, in the workplace, and in all other environments. But of particular concern is the meaning of joy and pleasure in relation to schooling and learning.

It is interesting to note that young children find great pleasure in recalling the joyful occasions they have experienced. This recall activity continues throughout a lifetime, and many adults can describe the favorite games of their childhood days. They can recite rhymes and jingles, sing the songs, give detailed procedures of their play activities, and share a host of memory gems related to spelling words, recalling dates of events, and other pertinent information as a result of joyful experiences they've had as children.

If one look closely at children who are involved in successful learning, facial expression, body tone, movement and buoyancy, posture, and a sense of aliveness are rather obvious indicators of feelings of joy. And listening carefully to what they have to say reveals other indicators such as feelings of gladness, enthusiasm, optimism, delight, satisfaction, self-esteem, and self-confidence.

Dr. Willard Gaylin, a leading American psychoanalayst, provides some interesting information about feelings of joy and

19

pleasure. He states

> Psychiatry . . . has always been more successful in dealing with pain than pleasure, sickness than health. I suspect that in most fields of scholarship it is easier to analyze what has gone wrong than what went right. Failure is analyzed, while success is merely enjoyed. (1, p. 200*)

There is a need for the different fields of scholarship to develop greater insights into the factors that contribute to individual enjoyment, particularly in relation to schooling and learning. Such insights might give new directions to schooling and might reduce—or even eliminate—much of the alienation that so many students are now developing as they progress into secondary education.

CATEGORIES OF PLEASURE

Dr. Gaylin presents an analysis of pleasure and joy by describing seven different categories of such feelings, each of which has implications for the education field and for the education of young children (2).

Stimulation: The Pleasure of Our Senses

The senses of taste, smell, touch, sound, and sight are presented as the simplest and most basic category of the feelings of joy and pleasure. Many educators do work to develop and heighten awareness in young children of the senses. However, the joy that can be experienced from the refinement and enlargement of sense perceptions suggests the need for even greater educational efforts to ensure that this avenue of access to learning will be a primary concern of the educational program.

---

*Numbers in parentheses appearing in the text refer to the References on page 79.

Discovery

The natural curiosity of young children and their continual desire to explore, handle, experiment, and examine can lead to a kind of pleasure that goes beyond the stimulation of the physical senses. Evidence reveals that the natural curiosity of children begins to diminish as they grow older. However, educators realize the great benefits children experience (including joy) when they individually make discoveries, and understand or find something new. The judicious use of the discovery approach can ensure joyful and pleasurable experiences when learning is designed for that purpose.

Expansion/Mastery

This category of feelings issues from recognition of personal growth and improvement. As children show improvement in physical and thinking skills and recognize that they have made progress, the realization of their improvement results in feelings of pleasure and joy. Solving puzzles in shorter periods of time, jumping higher, successful use of logical reasoning in solving mathematical problems, and many other kinds of challenges that require greater physical and mental nimbleness can build self-esteem and a sense of well-being. Hence, education should be designed to guide children to expand upon earlier understandings with greater levels of refinement.

Creativity

Creative imagination is presented as another category of human activity through which feelings of pleasure and joy can be derived. Researchers report that creative imagination peaks in young children at about the age of four and one-half years and then begins to decline. Knowing this, learning environments need to be designed to help reverse the trend. But what is creativity? To give precision to the use of the word later in this monograph, the following working definition is provided for early childhood education.

> Creativity is a process of combining known factors (knowledge, skills) into new relationships to produce new results—a new product, a new way of thinking and perceiving, a new way of performing. (3)

Children need learning environments in which they can use the knowledge and skills they acquire for new explorations and experiments to produce new ideas and new ways of doing things. Hence, educational activities should be designed to place children in creative environments that will stimulate original uses of their acquired knowledge and skills.

Immersion

The freedom of an indeterminable period of time for total immersion in a project of personal interest can become another source of feelings of pleasure and joy. Becoming totally immersed is described as "losing oneself" in pursuit of an enjoyable activity. Regular schooling practice normally does not provide young children with opportunities to reach a level of oblivion to time and the school schedule. A building activity with blocks, art work with colors and clay, playing house and dressing, imaginative cooking, lego-type materials, cutting pictures from magazines for "my book," and many other similar kinds of activities have possibilities for immersion and deriving feelings of joy and pleasure.

Fusion with People

Identification with a larger group—and recognizing that it was the cooperative effort of individual members that resulted in the group's success—is another category of feelings of pleasure. An individual "enlargement" results from joining in with others to accomplish things. The individual joy and pleasure realized from fusion with others through small-and large-group activity is a category of great importance to early childhood programs. The thrill derived from cooperative effort with others can enhance learning and provide another source of joy for young children.

Transcendental Experience

Dr. Gaylin (1) points out that the sixth category "fusion with people" helps us to understand the seventh, "transcendental experience." This latter category is presented as a form of pleasure associated with the feeling of being lifted out of oneself, of being a part of a larger order of things. It is explained as an enlargement of self, a sense of continuity beyond existence; confrontation with nature is suggested as a common source of this kind of experience. This form of pleasure and joy is derived from a sense of being a member of the universe or cosmos. Transcendental experience is perhaps the most challenging of the seven categories from which to draw relationships with early childhood education. However, perhaps the group, school, community, city, state, country, and world membership concept that begins to form in the early years can lay the foundation for expanding an understanding of this category of feelings in later years and thus become an even more realistic source for generating feelings of joy and pleasure.

JOY THEORY

A joy theory in learning is implied by the seven categories of feelings of pleasure described above. The joy and pleasure children can derive from learning is not merely an experience of those children whose homes are bastions of good will and exemplars of nurturing and caring. Different levels of joy can be experienced by all children in many school activities, regardless of home conditions. Joy can be desired, planned for, sought after, stimulated, encouraged, prompted, and realized when it is a primary goal of educational activity. But what causes joy to actually happen in the educational experience of children? Is it made possible by the physical setting in which learning takes place? By the learning environment? By the curriculum programs and materials used? By district-stated goals and administrative directives? By teachers in the delivery of learning programs? By other factors?

Every aspect of schooling (e.g., schedule, lighting, temperature, physical setting, custodial provisions, learning environments, attitudes of total school staff, curriculum materials, administrative control, equipment and supplies, home lives of children and staff) can have an influence on the learning activities of young children. This monograph is concerned, however, with what is believed to be the single, greatest influence on children's successful and joyful learning in a complex educational system—the teacher. The teacher ultimately spells the success or failure of learning regardless of the favorable or unfavorable conditions under which learning takes place. Teachers—even when working under the most adverse conditions—have been known to be highly successful in guiding children to find delight in learning and joy in life in general. Even the best school programs and the most carefully researched and designed sets of curriculum materials will not be successful without the guidance of a teacher who has that magic twinkle in the eye, who loves children, who is committed to helping children learn and enjoy schooling. How great is the task of teachers of young children!

Chapter 4

THE TEACHER'S ROLE IN JOYFUL LEARNING

There is probably no greater source of joy for those involved in schooling than teachers with a burning desire to guide children in learning, whose study and preparation have resulted in a beautiful weave of knowledge about children (including child development principles) and subject area content, who have tested and refined their instructional skills. Such teachers have little difficulty engaging children in exciting and pleasurable educational ventures. Teachers who are truly prepared to guide the educational development of children will have an inner joy of assurance that can be contagious—both to colleagues and to children. A teacher who does not enjoy teaching—or who does not enjoy teaching because of lack of preparation—will fail to infuse children with joy. All successful teachers will happily admit that their best days were those when their preparation and general alertness were of such quality that joyful learning could be anticipated and even assured. Teachers who consistently "wing it," and use the same set of established procedures year after year, will be devoid of the freshness of professional life that invigorates and generates new feelings of satisfaction and joy with oneself.

CHARACTERISTICS OF SUCCESSFUL TEACHERS

What are the characteristics of successful early childhood teachers? The successful teacher is a thoughtful planner of educational encounters—encounters designed to bring together learners, knowledge (content), and instructors into effective relationships for teaching and learning. But a successful early childhood teacher is also—

- A dialog leader
- A facilitator of communication and symbol systems unique to the different curricular and noncurricular areas
- A facilitator and exemplar of child development principles
- An observer, selecter, and user of developmentally appropriate language, vocabulary, and learning materials
- A nurturer of young children who need the reassurance that only a supportive and consistent guide and helper can provide (a kind of parent)
- A patient and articulate listener.
- A consultant and adviser who is available to assist children with all matters related to schooling (a kind of psychologist and counselor)
- A mediator who ensures that fair play and equality exists among the children in the group (a judicious intervener)
- A stimulator of new ideas
- A provider of and believer in the value of educational play (a kind of playmate)
- An encourager of creative imagination
- A collaborator with parents to effectively extend learning beyond the classroom
- A professional who is dedicated and enjoys bringing joy to children through educational activity.

Early childhood educators have many professional expectations, and their success is dependent upon filling the many different roles needed daily in the life of a child.

DESIGN OF EDUCATIONAL ENCOUNTERS

Educational encounters are the designs for educational activity resulting from bringing together information about learners, instructors, and knowledge (content) into a well-honed and orchestrated whole for teaching and learning. Oftentimes learning activities are organized solely on the basis of teacher perceptions of children's needs and interests without giving attention to knowledge and instructional concerns. At other times instruction may be driven by a cherished *methodology* without any reflection on children's expressed needs or the content to be presented. And at still other times teachers may submit to *content teaching* in complete disregard of learner and instructional considerations. Educational encounters will be far more successful, particularly over an extended period of time, when equal and studied attention are given by the teacher/designer to learner, instructional, and knowledge considerations. All three are important to providing the best educational experiences for young children, and the potential for enjoyable learning will be increased significantly when a dependence of one upon the other is established.

Learner Considerations

The teacher/designer needs to know as much as possible about the backgrounds of learners to ensure the appropriateness of the educational experience. Teacher perceptions of children's interests and needs are important and must be identified for the successful planning of educational encounters. Teachers should consider the following in developing their knowledge base for planning an education program:

- Have the perceptions of interests and needs been validated through observation and discussion with young children?
- What research data concerning developmental stages

27

and age and grade groupings are available that should be considered in planning educational encounters for young children?

- Which learning theories concerning young children are important to know about?
- Which learning theories seem to be appropriate for a specific group of children?
- Which special characteristics of the children's social and economic backgrounds are important to consider in planning?
- What societal expectations are there for young children in a particular community or district?
- What is the nature of earlier programs in which the children have participated?
- What are the entry achievement levels of the children in a group that have relevance to a particular educational program?
- Which learning principles are important to consider in the design of educational encounters for young children?
- What information about the children is available that gives clues for stimulating joyful participation in learning?

These and other questions are important for the teacher/designer to ask in learning as much information as possible about a group of children in order to determine how best to present a selected program and its content.

Knowledge Considerations

Background and experience in the knowledge structures of the subjects to be presented (and even in nonschool subjects such as household chores, caring for siblings, technologies used in the home, games and sports activities, community functions) is a prerequisite for the successful planning of educational encounters. In this connection, teachers should consider the following:

- What are the types of knowledge and their structures or taxonomies?
- What data are available to substantiate the need to follow a given sequence for presentation of the structures to young children?
- What attendant skills need to be developed for successful use of knowledge by young children?
- Is it possible to identify linkages between knowledge in the different subject areas (or nonsubject areas) and to determine how these linkages can best be approached in planning for instruction?
- Is there value for young children in establishing relationships between knowledge areas in different subjects and in nonsubjects?
- How much of what should be presented and at what intervals?
- What knowledge should be withheld until later based upon the perceived developmental levels of the children in a specific group?
- Is a recommended sequence for presenting knowledge available?
- In what ways does the presentation of knowledge relate to enjoyable learning?

These and other questions are appropriate for pondering the planning process. Most of the questions asked in relation to knowledge considerations can be answered satisfactorily only by having sufficient background information about learners.

Instructional Considerations

This area is primarily concerned with the nature of teachers and what they need to know in designing and presenting educational encounters for young children.

- What teacher resources are available to assist in the instructional process (paraprofessionals, community resource persons, subject area specialists)?
- What instructional strategies and methodologies have proved to be developmentally appropriate for young children?
- What methodologies and strategies are inherent within specific subject areas, and which ones could be universally applied to all subjects?
- What materials, supplies, and equipment are essential to the successful implementation of the encounters?
- What special facilities or spaces in the school are needed to implement the planned encounters?
- Is there an effective and tested evaluation plan that takes into consideration the backgrounds of the children, the nature of the knowledge and skills to be developed, and the appropriateness of the methodologies and strategies to be employed?
- What other aspects of instruction must be considered in the design workable encounters for young children that consider the backgrounds of learners and the knowledge to be presented?
- In what ways can methodologies and stretegies be adapted to promote joyful learning?

Questions such as these will have useful answers only when they are considered within the context of learner and knowledge considerations.

What do educational encounters have to do with joyful experience in learning for young children? It is believed that when appropriate attention is given to learner, knowledge, and instructional considerations, there will be less likelihood of something going wrong when the encounters are implemented. When things "click" and fit together nicely, even very young children recognize what is happening. The goal is to help young children experience success in educational encounters—a sure source of joy in education. When things do not work well there is a strong possibility that feelings of defeat, disenchantment, and discouragement will supplant the desired feelings of accomplishment and joy. The design, development, implementation, and assessment of educational encounters will greatly influence whether children experience feelings of joy in learning or whether their inclination to learn will become dampened.

TEACHER LANGUAGE/DIALOG

Characteristics of the successful early childhood teacher presented earlier are that he/she is an observer, selecter, and user of developmentally appropriate language, vocabulary, and learning materials. Using developmentally appropriate language, vocabulary, and visual symbols is a very important responsibility of the teacher for both reading and nonreading children. For the young child, words, symbols, and language are relational, and without relatedness to practical experience they become nonfunctional. Words used in contexts related to children's levels of understanding and past or present experience can become permanent entries in their expanding vocabulary. A teacher who uses language and words beyond the comprehension level of children creates frustration, alienation, and a joyless school experience. As children's experiences are broadened, the introduction of words that represent something they have understood is fun and enjoyable. The words may later be misused, but the trial and error system is a valuable preparatory experience in language learning.

Vocabulary expansion and symbol recognition are basic to children's future learning at each higher grade level. Therefore, pacing is the key to success. Too much (or not enough), too fast (or too slow), at levels beyond the comprehension of young

31

children—or unrelated to experiences they are capable of comprehending—will breed confusion. Collaboration with experienced early childhood colleagues in relation to a specific group of children, or to individual children, will provide valuable clues to what is developmentally appropriate language and vocabulary. The successful use of symbols, words, and language by children is directly related to the level of joy they will experience in educational activities. Abstractions (the use of words or symbols without relational understandings) are not satisfying to young children. But hearing words used by others and then trying them out is a natural response, a response that builds acquaintance with new sounds and pronunciations. The instructional process, however, requires much more than a generalized experience devoid of relational meanings.

The early childhood teacher is *a dialog leader*. It is prudent dialog used throughout each school day that stimulates thinking, energizes the intellect, launches children into new learning adventures, guides them to successful conclusions, and resets the stage for sequential and related new adventures. The early childhood teacher participates as a side coach, a prompter, and provides dialog that—

1. Suggests directions without giving all directions,
2. Asks questions that stimulate thought without giving all the answers,
3. Suggests realistic alternative approaches when roadblocks are experienced,
4. Encourages effort toward completion or resolution rather than premature termination, and
5. Reinforces children's work in a positive way to prevent alienation and ensure an open mind to learning in the future.

Teachers of young children need to learn when their dialog is too much or too little. Too much can achieve the effect of a radio playing in the background without anyone within its hearing range attending to its sound. Too little can leave children stymied and perplexed without knowing where to turn next—a very distraughtful experience for a young learner. This important area of performance should be of great concern and receive much analysis and study, for it is often teacher language and dialog that has a negative impact on children's learning and eliminates all hope for an enjoyable school experience.

ORCHESTRATION/DELIVERY

Personal study and preparation, in-depth knowledge and understanding of children and how they learn, good learning programs and materials, thoughtful and intensive planning, and aspirations to be successful all contribute to the refinement of educational encounters. A nonchalant approach with low expectations for children and a "winging it is sufficient"attitude will reduce or even negate the best preparation. Successful teaching of young children requires as much delicacy and refining of planning and as a successful performance by a symphony orchestra. The orchestration of educational encounters—a combining of all parts into a cohesive, related, connective, and harmonious whole—is a major influence on the success of all educational activity. But even with the finest personal background and planning possible, the actual delivery of the encounters to children is the ultimate quality test.

The manner in which education is presented will influence the degree of joy experienced by children. Of all the related parts of the process of education, delivery is one of the most important. Some of the factors that affect delivery are—

1. The stimulation and intrigue suggested by the teacher
2. The method of introducing the encounter
3. The teacher attitude displayed in initiating activity
4. The continuing concern of the teacher for each child throughout the encounter

5. The nature of the side coaching and questions provided by the teacher
6. The availability of all essential materials and supplies
7. The respect established by children for each other that ensures a favorable work and learning environment.

Adequate space in which to work, and other aspects may also affect the success of the delivery. It is primarily through delivery that the groundwork for joy must be laid and then promoted.

As suggested earlier, feelings of joy can be stimulated, planned for, sought after, encouraged, and prompted, and this is realized through teacher delivery of educational encounters. A successful teacher is much like an actor who internalizes a script and then uses it effectively while acting out the actions it implies. There are also numerous occasions for improvising additional script and actions to accommodate situations that occur as the needs of individual children become evident. Although teaching is a form of acting, the believable and successful teacher of young children is one whose script and actions are felt to issue from the heart of a caring and nurturing person whose performance exemplifies sincerity and authenticity.

ASSESSMENT OF JOY IN LEARNING

The introspective early childhood teacher periodically will spend time reflecting on the program presented to children in order to assess the effectiveness of each of its parts. Review and analysis in terms of children's progress, and the degree to which each part has contributed to their progress, can lead to program improvement. Hence, the goal of such assessments is diagnostic—the identification of areas to improve that will have a positive impact on children's long-range success and enjoyment in learning.

The teacher is perhaps the most critical part of the total program, and teacher self-assessment should be the beginning point of program evaluation. It is reasonable to assume that if the teacher has not found the total educational experience to be enjoyable, there likely will be little difference in the way the children feel. It is helpful to enlist the assistance of other early childhood teachers in the assessment process to validate personal impressions. But what are the other parts of a program that influence children's progress?

Leadership within the school, staff support, scheduling and time allotment, space availability, budget and allocations, resource and support personnel availability, equipment availability and upkeep, consumable materials and supplies availability, overall physical setting, curriculum materials, group size, parental support, and other such parts of the program relate to the total impact of the educational experience. When assessments reveal that one or more parts are negatively impacting children's progress, corrective measures need to be taken. Programs that are not assessed periodically usually limp along without the ailment being diagnosed, and few clues are available to suggest what to do next.

As posited earlier, there is little doubt that when all of the parts of a program work well and fit together, a harmonious feeling will be generated among all participants. The experience provided by a well-organized and orchestrated set of program elements will have a positive influence on children's level of enjoyment, their interest in learning, and in being a full participant in the program.

Chapter 5

ESTABLISHING ENJOYABLE EDUCATIONAL CLIMATES

LEARNING ENVIRONMENTS

Learning environments are defined in several ways by educators. One definition refers to children's expanded environment as they progress from home care to participation as a student in school. The geographical range of their life environment is expanded beyond the home, the number of people within their new environment is expanded as they establish relationships with a larger number of people and develop new friendships, and the roles through which they participate in learning are expanded. Another definition refers to what some call *learning centers*. Each center is a kind of learning environment with materials, equipment, furnishings, and visual aids that correspond to the center's purpose. These are usually organized either for one child or for pairs or small groups of children. A third definition refers to the physical setting (light, temperature, outside noise intrusion, furnishings [hardness, softness], colors, spaces, etc.) of learning areas used by children.

EDUCATIONAL CLIMATES

In this chapter learning environments will be referred to as *educational climates*. These are concerned with the atmosphere, conditions, mood, tone, and other settings that teachers establish for learning, whether it is in centers, in free play in the classroom or on the playground, in large group activity, or in any other kind of organization or grouping appropriate for early childhood education. The kinds of educational climates that teachers establish have much to do with whether children enjoy both learning and the total school experience.

Educational Climates That Can Result in Learner Disenchantment

To become enchanted with something is to become attracted, intrigued, or captivated by it, anticipating a kind of thrill, delight, or fascination because of the interest it generates and the attention it elicits for a period of time. Learning activities designed for children should have enchanting qualities. There are educational climates, however, that lack these qualities and result in disenchantment. Several such climates were mentioned briefly in Chapter 2, "Child Development." Following are some of the more general kinds of climates that can lead to learner disenchantment among young children.

- Conditions that stifle original thinking and creative imagination
- Social pressure to stop imagining and be realistic
- Too many rote and recall activities and an overemphasis on memorization
- Lack of opportunities to engage in problem solving and decision making activities
- Strict control during learning and play activities that prohibits questioning and exploration
- Conditions that result from children becoming fearful of trying a new approach
- Holding a group of children back for evidence of desired levels of readiness
- Placing too high value on conformity in all activities
- A lack of routines and too many rigid, routinely organized tasks
- Too much group work; too little individual work
- Approval of only those behaviors that follow established traditions
- Activities that require too much or too little stress

- Required exploration of a problem to the point that motivation subsides and the problem no longer presents new possibilities
- Physical environments that give an impression of being physically or psychologically unsafe.

Introspective teachers need to develop a constant alertness to climates that result in children becoming disenchanted with learning. As joyless faces begin to appear, an analysis of the conditions set for learning could prove to give good insights into what led to disenchantment and what remedies need to be initiated to ensure joyful learning in the future.

Friendly Educational Climates

A friendly educational climate invites, attracts, encourages, appeals, generates interest, and evokes a kind of magnetism that draws children into learning activites. It is interesting to note that when children anticipate that joy will be an outcome of their involvement, it is not difficult to enlist their full participation. The finest preparations for learning can be made with all related elements woven into a workable design for delivery to children, but the educational climate established can spell the success or failure of even the best designs. Following are some features of educational climates that are friendly and nonthreatening for children.

- Many opportunites to contribute original ideas
- Freedom to share differing points of view
- Freedom and encouragement to seek new ways to solve problems
- Freedom to explore and use different areas and materials in the room
- Establishment of an appropriate degree of stress
- Sense of approval for keeping fantasies alive

- Help in developing inquiry skills
- A degree of informality that ensures freedom to change roles
- Feeling of trust and equality among all children in the group
- Assurance that enjoyable learning is a goal of all educational activity
- Opportunities for convergent and divergent thinking
- Sense of "ownership" of the school.

An appropriate level of stress is believed to be very important in young children's learning; too little stress can result in their failing to focus problems and tasks, while too much stress can generate feelings of rigidity. A degree of stress is needed to stimulate innovative thinking, but accompanying it must be sufficient security to offset the anxiety that uncertainly brings.

Convergent thinking is also important to the learning of young children. Children need to learn to approach a problem while being limited to existing methods and knowledge, relying only on facts already known. They also need the experience of approaching a problem by searching for links between past experience and something they have not previously considered. This approach permits thinking to go in many directions while producing a range of possible solutions. This *reaching into the unknown* is referred to as divergent thinking. Both kinds of thinking are extremely valuable in establishing learning patterns in the early years.

Educational Climates Supportive of Developmentally Appropriate Challenges

The value of stress in children's learning relates to establishing educational climates that present developmentally appropriate challenges. Any kind of challenge, if accepted,

40

presents a level of stress that spurs inquisitiveness, determination, mustering of energy, and action. Children need challenges, but the challenges must be appropriate to their age, maturation, and background level.

Learner considerations were discussed earlier as one of three kinds of considerations essential to planning successful educational encounters for children. Knowledge and instructional considerations must be adapted to what is known about the developmental levels of learners. Working within the context of these three considerations will provide insight into presenting appropriate challenges to young children.

The "Position Statement on Developmentally Appropriate Practices in Programs for 4- and 5-Year-Olds" prepared by the National Association for the Education of Young Children (4) presents a summary of appropriate and inappropriate practices in the areas of curriculum goals, teaching strategies, guidance of socioemotional development, language development and literacy, cognitive development, physical development, aesthetic development, parent-teacher relations, assessment of children, program entry, teacher qualifications, and staffing. The entries for several of the areas imply needed climates for presenting developmentally appropriate challenges for young children. But what do educational climates have to do specifically with developmentally appropriate challenges?

The acceptance of a challenge and the pursuit of its resolution should be accompanied by a climate that is supportive. As children assume responsibility for the challenges they accept, they need the assurance that they will be working in a friendly learning climate with the guidance of a loving and caring teacher. Following are some other features of educational climates that are essential for children to sense as they are presented with appropriate challenges.

- Understanding that acceptance of a challenge will contribute to personal growth and development

41

- Realization that the challenges presented are commensurate with their individual capabilities
- Adequate time will be provided to reach resolutions in a positive setting
- Knowledge that a helpful teacher guide will always be available to listen and provide suggestions when roadblocks are experienced
- Belief established that not all challenges may be completely resolved and that other opportunities will be available in the future (reduction of stress due to anticipated failure)
- Freedom to ask questions, express concerns, and share problems without fear of punishment
- A positive, consistent support system
- A teacher who is sufficiently flexible and adapts to changes that benefit the learner
- Reassurance of a safe and nonthreatening climate for pursuing challenges
- Assurance that everything needed to meet a challenge will be provided
- Teacher determination to enjoy teaching and make learning enjoyable for children.

Supportive climates are a source of joy and inspiration for young children. Knowing that a caring and helpful teacher is nearby is a settling influence on young lives. With this kind of support system, young children will pursue learning happily and willingly, with a desire to learn and be cooperative.

Chapter 6

PLAY: IMPORTANCE
TO JOY IN LEARNING

Young children's lives from their toddler days have been saturated with many different forms of play. They play with toys, household items, clothing, siblings, adults, and even with food. They are able to find some play function for just about anything within their immediate environment. A goal of early education should be to utilize the creative play instincts of young children in planning learning activities. Learning approached as play will make a far greater impact on children's development than learning conceived as a process of sitting at a table or desk passively completing an assignment. A play orientation to learning for young children makes learning significantly more enjoyable.

Froebel called a school for four- and five-year-old children a *kindergarten,* (a garden for children). Maria Montessori stated that in "more modern and better schools, those that correspond to Froebel's ideals, the educators behave as do good gardeners and cultivators towards their plants" (5). The cultivation of children should proceed from where they are, from their play-oriented lives, building upon their existing childlike instincts as they develop into more mature thinkers and doers.

Descriptions of several kinds of play are provided next as general categories that have some relationship to each other. The categories presented are intended as a "mixed set"; that is, they share elements in common and are not clearly distinguishable from each other. The intent here is to present some of the more familiar language used when describing different kinds of play that suggest a special focus for both learning and enjoyment.

DRAMATIC PLAY

Winifred Word, in the first sentence in her book *Playmaking with Children,* states that "what children do is more significant to them than what they see and hear" (6). Young children need many opportunities to *do,* to participate in make-believe play, and to use their energies *doing* real, live actions. Dramatizing the movements and sounds of an animal, portraying a robot, conversing with an imaginary companion, flying across the room like an airplane, galloping about on a broomstick horse, improvising dialog between two inanimate objects, and other such play-living is valuable to the development of language and thinking skills. Make-believe play, story dramatization, impromptu and rehearsed pantomime, shadow and puppet (hand, finger) play, and all other forms of extemporaneous drama should have a place in the daily learning of children.

IMITATIVE PLAY

Much of what children learn in their early years is from imitation of things observed in the environment and imitation of the behavior of older children and adults. Sounds in the environment (sirens, wind, animals), sounds and movements of motorized vehicles and equipment, and other things that attract children's attention are often imitated as a form of play. This play form is valuable to children's development as they *try out* and *invent* sounds and actions that they believe to be adequate representations of what they have observed. They also imitate each other, and in every imitative effort they learn new information and skills. Imitation is a valuable experience for children that expands their play instincts and serves as a stimulator of cognitive development as well as a source of enjoyment.

SYMBOLIC PLAY

In symbolic play children use an object of their choice to represent something else. Oftentimes the object selected is lacking in similarity to what a child decides it represents. An empty can may be used both as a telephone receiver and speaker, a carrot as a water pistol, a hollow cardboard tube as a sword, an empty cup used to give a doll a drink of water. There are usually no rules children observe in symbolic play; anything can represent anything else of their choosing.

Symbolic play should be encouraged. Children need to be challenged to find things to play with that they believe can be used to represent something else. In doing so, creative imagination is stimulated and the activity becomes a source of pleasure for children. This kind of play extends thinking beyond the general limits of conformity and encourages higher level thinking skills.

SPONTANEOUS PLAY

Spontaneous play provides children freedom to pursue personal interests at their own pace without being directed by a predetermined set of educational objectives. Children need daily opportunities to follow their play instincts, to wander about, to look, to explore, to try out different things that catch their attention, to imitate others, to sit quietly, to run, and to daydream. There is always a tendency to hurry children, to make certain they are doing at every moment what the educator considers to be productive. The purpose of spontaneous play is to "let it happen" without the influence of a teacher. It is believed that through spontaneous play children synthesize much of the information they have learned previously and begin to understand its practical applications.

As children become involved, the teacher should take advantage of opportunities to *briefly* enter a child's activity for one-to-one dialog. The goal is to let the child tell what is happening, why the play activity is enjoyable. It provides a child with *tell time*, with the teacher relegated to *listen time*. This helps the child to develop independent thinking skills. Spontaneity in play is the goal, and teachers need to respect children's rights to pursue personal interests independently.

RITUAL PLAY

Routinely planned activities and events are important in the education of young children. People of all ages need and appreciate certain routines in life, but excessive use of routines in education can evolve into a kind of ritualistic system that will be devoid of freshness and learning to become familiar with new processes and skills.

Ritual play is the kind of play that children like to do because it is familiar and they can predict a degree of success with it. This kind of play has value, and children should be given time to follow its appeal. Some children are hesitant (for a variety of reasons) to step into the unknown independently and go beyond their established play routines. It is important therefore for the teacher to introduce children to other kinds of play, to other possibilities that will help them broaden their interests. The goal is to preserve those areas of learning where children are successful, but to guide them beyond "where they are" and present new challenges and opportunities that will expand their possibilities for enjoyment in learning.

EXPERIMENTAL PLAY

Experimental play is a play form in which children pursue play-oriented activities that are unfamiliar to them. Age-appropriate materials and objects are provided and children are invited to explore them independently, to learn their characteristics, and to determine their possible uses. They are encouraged to learn whether the materials and objects have sound-producing capabilities, are usable in building things, can be used to represent other things, suggest a story that could be told, or have special characteristics that make playing with them enjoyable. The goal is to give children the freedom to experiment with the materials and objects at their own pace for the period of time that interest is maintained. Sharing the results of their experiments with other children causes them to reflect on their experiences; it also provides a good foundation for later experimental play.

SUMMARY

There are many other forms of play that have been described by different writers. Constructive play, cognitive play, random play, water play, sand play, block play, cooperative play, pretend play, fantasy play, practice play, make-believe play, and shadow play are some of the more prominent forms. There are obvious similarities and relationships between many of those mentioned here and the six briefly described above. Teachers who may wish to study the subject of play will find the following publications to be helpful.

Forman, G. E., and Hill, F. *Constructive Play: Applying Piaget in the Preschool.* Menlo Park, Calif.: Addison-Wesley, 1984.

Hyde, D. M. G. *Piaget and Conceptual Development.* New York: Holt, Rinehart and Winston, 1970.

Labinowicz, E. *The Piaget Primer.* Menlo Park, Calif.: Addison-Wesley, 1980.

Rogers, C. S., and Sawyers, J. K. *Play in the Lives of Children.* Washington, D.C.: National Association for the Education of Young Children, 1988.

Chapter 7

PRESENTING CONTENT IN AN ENJOYABLE WAY

Children enjoy learning new content in the subject areas. They enjoy developing new skills using the knowledge they gain. When learning activities are designed to be appropriate to the age and background experience of young children, the problem some refer to as "push-down academics" does not occur. Many who argue this issue in early childhood education place themselves in one of two unfortunate positions—no subject area content to be presented, or content to be presented in a way that follows the traditional pattern found in elementary schools. There is an important third position that needs to be considered. When content is presented in an interesting, enjoyable, sequential, age-appropriate, and play-oriented way, learning becomes exciting for children. Content learning is a source of joy in a child's life when it is interesting, when it is related to and broadens and extends earlier learnings, when gamelike activities are used to present it, and when it is planned according to their current level of understanding and skill development.

KNOWLEDGE STRUCTURES

Knowledge structures for an early childhood program are developed by selecting content from the subject areas believed to be appropriate for children at several age-developmental levels (e.g., children ages 3–5, 4–7, 3–8, grades K–3, K–6, K–12). It is essential that the selection be made for children at several levels to have some indication of which parts at age four, for example, will relate to age three and age five and beyond. Selections of content should be made by those who have an in-depth

49

understanding of a subject area and experience in teaching the subject to children.

It is oftentimes best first to compile an array of subject area content from which specific elements will be drawn to create knowledge structures. From this array, a structure begins to take form as elements are selected and arranged into a chronology for presentation (simple to complex, concrete to abstract). This way of structuring knowledge will lead to its sequential presentation. When knowledge is presented in a logical way, fundamental learnings will serve as bases for introducing more complex learnings, over a period of time, that correspond to the age-developmental levels of children. Sequential learning is superior to the approach that currently exists in many early childhood programs—an approach that consists of the random selection of content without giving consideration to an overall design that has a chronology that has been determined by experienced practitioners and theorists in the field. When guided in learning by a program that has some kind of systematic chronology that establishes *relatedness* between what is learned at lower and higher levels, the experience will be enjoyable for children. Even very young children recognize the value of and enjoy learning that has an obvious relationship to something previously learned.

Consider the following example for creating a knowledge structure for children ages three to five in the subject area generally referred to as social studies. First, is an example of an array of principal knowledge areas compiled to represent social studies.

1. Community
2. Rules and laws
3. Geography
4. Safety
5. Money
6. Place and space
7. Human events
8. Economics

Next, elements for each of the principal knowledge areas within the array are compiled.

Community

cooperative group activity
responsibilities of family members
names of individuals within the school community
responsibilities of school staff members and helpers
awareness of roles of community leaders
offices held by elected officials

Rules and Laws

value of rules to family and group success
fairness in school activities and playing areas
traffic and safety rules
formulation of rules for games and class activities

Geography

home address (street, city), telephone number
location of employment for father and/or mother
directional vocabulary (up-down, left-right, nearby-far away,
    above-below, in front-behind, on each side)
relative size vocabulary (short-tall, high-low, large-small,
    tiny-huge, wide -narrow, long-short)
representational aspects of maps, globes, models
simple maps
weather in relation to names of places in world
time as a progression of events (clock, days, months,
    sequence of events)

Safety

safe and unsafe areas in school, playgrounds, home,
    neighborhood
rules of safety in school, playgrounds, home, neighborhood
safety procedures
threats to safety
safety symbols in school, community
traffic lights

Money

care of money and personal property
coins (penny, nickel, dime, quarter, half dollar, one dollar bill)
saving and securing money

Place and Space

sharing things in school
storage areas for equipment and materials
storage and retrieval systems for equipment and materials

Human Events

principal holidays, special days (what they represent)
names and days of months of the year
birthdays of family members, classmates, and persons of
   historical significance

Economics

basic economical needs (food, clothing, shelter)
ownership (personal and shared community property)
economical needs (how they are met)

These lists of elements could be reduced, adapted, expanded, and/or replaced according to the needs determined to be essential for laying a good foundation for social studies in early childhood education. When the elements for the principal areas have been determined, the next step would be to arrange them according to a chronology for presentation. For instance, under *community*, learning to be cooperative in group activity would be presented long before learning about the offices held by elected officials, and under *human events*, principal holidays would precede learning about persons of historical significance. Some of the elements would likely need to be adapted to complete a chronology from more simple to more complex sets of ideas to be presented to children. The important point in designing knowledge structures is to conceive a plan whereby relationships between the elements are shown so that things being learned will be linked to things to be learned earlier and things to be learned later.

This same procedure could be used for creating knowledge structures that will ensure sequentiality in other subject areas such as science, mathematics, language, art, music, and movement/physical education. The appropriateness of knowledge from any subject cannot be determined until it is known what the structure of knowledge is. Too many decisions are made concerning this issue by hiding beneath a cloak of developmental appropriateness without sufficient background in the structures of knowledge to be presented and how the structures are best learned by young children. Developmental appropriateness and knowledge structures must be examined together; the best judgments will be made when the two are considered as interdependent.

THE CURRICULUM APPROACH

The concern expressed for developing knowledge structures is presented as support for insightful curriculum planning in early childhood education. A good, flexible curriculum design, with well-conceived curriculum materials, will always be a source of joy for both the children and the teacher. Such a program eliminates the randomness that occurs so many times when there is no design with supportive materials. A logical and organized presentation of knowledge from the subjects adds a high degree of *comfort* to the educational process for teachers and children.

CONCEPTUAL DEVELOPMENT
AND SEQUENTIALISM

Concepts in the subject areas are *generalizations that consist of a host of interrelated particulars.* As more and more particulars are learned, conceptual understanding is expanded. For instance, children's concept of *community* (see the knowledge structure for social studies) is expanded as they grow in their understanding of *cooperative group activity* (a particular) through many different kinds of small and large group experiences in their early years. They gradually learn that a community of any kind (school, home, neighborhood) is successful only to the degree that *members of the community accept responsibilities* (another particular) for its maintenance and wellness. Their acquaintances and friendships are expanded and their conception of a community is broadened as they gradually learn of the many others who accept responsibilities in the community. Gradually they learn about the need for leaders in a community, how the leaders are selected, what roles the leaders assume, how the community is organized, how it functions from day to day, the kind of economic support it needs to operate successfully, and many other similar particulars. This kind of expanded understanding of a host of interrelated particulars is referred to as conceptual development. Learning is never a burden to a young learner if it is developmentally appropriate and has a direct and practical relationship to life; the concept of community is one that continues to become enlarged in the learner's mind throughout a lifetime.

Learning in early childhood education through a conceptual development approach can establish sequentiality and a sense of authenticity and personal benefit to young learners. It enables the presentation of sets of related ideas that gradually become more complex and lead to more in-depth understandings throughout life. A conceptual approach is dependent upon the creation of knowledge structures within the subjects to be embraced in a program. A program that has such a well-conceived design will be a source of joy to all involved in the educational process. Concepts are the threads that create a sense of continuity in the minds of learners and provide a means for relating earlier learnings to later learnings.

CYCLICAL ORGANIZATION

In its simplest meaning *cyclical* refers to something that "comes around again and again." Or, as Bruner described many years ago, *a spiral curriculum* is one "that turns back on itself at higher levels" (7). At any educational level, learners enjoy having repeated and new experiences with something they have learned previously. A cyclical organization of content from the subjects requires a revisiting of ideas presented earlier, a kind of perpetual reinforcement of earlier learnings. Once the particulars of a concept are presented, they continue to reappear, even though new particulars are being introduced. No area of knowledge—once it is introduced—is abandoned or neglected; it continues to find space in learning activities at higher levels.

This kind of curriculum organization is helpful to children who may not have grasped the full meaning of ideas during an earlier experience. It is also helpful to those who may have participated in a different program in another school and have recently moved to a new area. But it especially contributes to the joy level of all learners as they have new opportunities to be successful with the familiar rather than being constantly bombarded with a raft of unfamiliar ideas—or being devoid of experience with any kind of structured or sequential learning. A cyclical presentation of knowledge is a logical process that gives *comfort* and *reassurance* to learners. A random curriculum approach lacks depth by failing to build upon related earlier learnings, proceeding into high levels of understanding.

CURRICULUM INTEGRATION

Curriculum integration has been a primary interest of educators for many years. A poll in 1988 identified curriculum integration as a top priority issue in American education. It is interesting to note, however, that there have been many programs identified as "integrated" during past years, particularly at the early childhood level. A recent publication of the

Association for Supervision and Curriculum Development (8) suggests that the failure of many attempts have been caused by the *potpourri approach* to integration—random samplings of knowledge being used without giving attention to the structures of knowledge inherent in the subjects.

Some attribute children's lack of joy in learning to the study of subjects in isolation from each other. This is based on the belief that piecemeal learning (in the subjects) does not provide children with sufficient background and systems of thought for establishing relevance with what they learn to the practical issues of life. Other claims are made that integrated programs will—

- Eliminate the storing up of inert facts
- Ensure an increase in learning by reducing the small units of information presented to children
- Provide holistic learning experiences rather than piecemeal learning
- Help learners become better equipped to communicate with each other
- Bring the development of critical thinking skills into the regular curriculum rather than present it as a separate area of study
- Facilitate knowledge application and synthesis
- Increase the power of the child's mind as it develops systems for organizing an array of facts into patterns.

Many other claims are made about the value of integrated programs, but there is little research data available supporting the claims.

Three *levels* of integration are believed to be important for consideration in designing educational programs for young children: *thematic* integration, *knowledge* integration, and *learner-initiated* integration.

Thematic Integration

This level traditionally involves the selection of information from the subjects believed to be useful in understanding a thematic idea such as *transportation.* A level of integration is achieved as information from the different subjects contributes to understanding of the selected theme. The transportation theme could be approached by—

- Singing songs about transportation (music)
- Drawing and coloring pictures of different forms of transportation (art)
- Participating in movement activities utilizing traffic patterns and signals (movement and physical education)
- Counting the cars of a train and classifying the cars by shape and color (mathematics)
- Learning about the different kinds of fuel needed for different vehicles to have locomotion (science and technology)
- Understanding environmental problems associated with the burning of fuel and its effect on people (social studies)
- Creating and telling stories about transportation (language)
- Learning safety precautions in using different forms of transportation (health).

These activities and others could help children increase their understanding of the importance of transportation in the lives of people, and a level of integration will occur in relation to the selected theme.

Knowledge Integration

A second level of integration is possible as connective

relationships (linkages, touch points) are established between knowledge areas in one subject and those in other subjects. A problem occurs in planning for integration at this level when an assumption is made that all knowledge areas from the different subjects relate to each other. Some knowledge areas do not have relationships with others, but it may be essential for children to learn them since they could be important to maintaining a sense of sequentialism in what is presented. It is therefore important in early childhood to present knowledge areas when they need to be presented to ensure sequential experience, but it also is important to use knowledge in an integrative design when there are obvious linkages and when there is a reason for doing it.

As suggested earlier in this chapter, it is important in the design of an early childhood education program to create knowledge structures for each of the subjects to be included. It is from a study of the structures that the possibilities for integrating knowledge become evident. For instance, children might become involved in comparing different lengths of string to help build understanding of *longer* and *shorter* (mathematics). They select several different lengths for use in finding out whether they can jump the lengths of the string pieces (movement and physical education). Varying lengths of voice sounds are explored to build an understanding of longer and shorter sounds, or duration (music). There is a natural relationship established between music, movement and physical education, and mathematics in regard to length and duration. Later, the idea of length could be associated with the study of time (longer, shorter) in science. Such connective relationships are believed to constitute knowledge integration.

Consider these knowledge areas from the subjects as possibilities for establishing connective relationships in an integrated approach to learning.

Science Wayfinding (mapping)

Movement and Physical Education Direction (zigzagged,

58

curved, diagonal)

Music Composition (sound piece)

Mathematics Paths (curved, straight, zigzagged lines)

Language Reading (visual perception)

Social Studies Geography (simple maps)

Art Line (straight, curved, jagged)

Learning to read and follow a map is an important foundational knowledge area in science. Children might learn to draw and read a map that shows the location of open spaces, furniture, and large equipment in their classroom. They could also create a map on a large, open floor area using tape or other material that requires those who follow it to jump, hop, and leap in specific directions (art, movement and physical education). A related activity in music would be to read a *musical map* consisting of symbols that represent a series of interesting sounds to be produced by various objects that have different timbres. A graphic map might be created on a large, open floor area using curved, zigzagged, straight, and curved lines that children could follow. They could take turns "running the course" to find out who can complete the course (map) in a shorter period of time (mathematics, art, movement and physical education, social studies). Perhaps these briefly described activities conjure up many other related activities that use knowledge areas in an integrative manner. There are obvious linkages between these knowledge areas from the subjects that offer possibilities for integrative experience. This is a much higher level of integration than that possible at the thematic level.

When there are natural relationships between the knowledge areas from the subjects, integrative learning is possible. It is very likely that children will find a higher degree of enjoyment participating in learning activities that are integrated.

The varied approaches to understanding a conceptual idea that transcends several subjects offers expanded experiences and presents a variety of ways to understand related areas of knowledge. Such a holistic approach to learning will benefit children more when this kind of approach is possible. But there will always be some knowledge areas in the subjects that will need to be presented independently of others because connective relationships are not always possible.

Learner-Initiated Integration

Another level of integration is the kind that learners do independently of formal educational settings or through direct instruction by a teacher-tutor. Children develop systems of thought (ways of thinking) from participation in good educational programs and sometimes from their parents. These systems often remain active in all of their future activities—at play, in the home, in the neighborhood, at the shopping center. Sometimes the experiences they have call to remembrance things they have learned, and their developing thinking skills cause them to independently relate the new experiences to past learnings. This assimilation of new information with information previously learned will, in many instances, establish connective relationships and result in integration.

Learning of this kind takes place in varying degrees among young children, but it is important for teachers of young children to remember that it can happen. Conducting discussions periodically while focusing on key concepts from the subjects presented earlier will often reveal an assimilation of new information with what was presented earlier. This is a reason why teachers need to spend time having one-to-one discussions with children to help them focus informally on what they have learned. Learner-initiated integration is probably the highest level of integration possible for a person of any age, and under the right conditions it will continue throughout life. There will always be enjoyment for the learner when it is possible to assimilate new information and advance independently in thinking skills and the use of new knowledge.

STYLES OF PRESENTATION

The importance of varying the methods and approaches for presenting learning activities to children has been alluded to earlier. People of all ages enjoy routines in life and a degree of regularity in their daily activities. But the desire for repeated experiences with the *familiar* does not mean newness and the unexpected are unappreciated in a child's life. Routines generate a feeling of security in children's lives and fulfill the need for familiarity in educational settings. A problem arises, however, when a teacher's selected styles of presentation do not meet the specific needs of all the children. An example of this problem follows.

A one-year research effort at the Carnegie-Mellon University's Children's School revealed differences between the preferred learning styles of boys and girls, ages three to five (9). The girls had little difficulty sitting on chairs at tables to work with materials. The boys perceived working at tables as difficult, and they did what they could to avoid the experience. The situation was finally diagnosed by the staff as "tableitis." Another style of presentation was tried by the staff and it was learned that the boys could do the same work as the girls if permitted to pursue it while sprawling, lying, or sitting on the floor. This is an example of using different approaches to planning learning activities for children in order to accommodate differences (whether real or imagined) that the children might have.

Leah Levinger and Jo Adler, in their article "How Children Learn," state: "No two children learn and develop in exactly the same way. Each has an individual style and pace. Even though children go through the same stages of development, it's not possible to know exactly at what point when your children

61

should be crawling, tying shoelaces, or reading *Moby Dick.*" (10).
This valuable article discusses things that affect learning and how parents can help. The individual differences of young children are very real. Parents and teachers who desire to push children "up" to the next stage of development they perceive as where the child should be can result in the child becoming disenchanted with learning. The styles of learning teachers employ have to be selected to accommodate a wide range of abilities and differences. The goal is to help each child become joyfully engaged in learning within a style of presentation where he/she will be capable of working and experiencing success.

Teachers are encouraged to observe young children closely to learn whether they are inclined toward the methods and approaches being used to engage them in learning activities. Even some of the most time-honored approaches of seasoned teachers may not accommodate the learning needs of all young children. Experimentation with approaches may reveal avoidance behaviors and signal the need for flexible styles of presentation. Matters such as location in the room, physical setting, placement near a child that others are avoiding, crowded conditions, noise interference, as well as a host of teacher methods and approaches should all be reviewed frequently to learn whether a condition has been created that is causing a child to resist participation in learning activities.

Chapter 8

JOY STIMULATORS IN LEARNING AND SCHOOLING

Some of a professional educator's most pleasurable experiences are the occasions one has to visit schools in our country and in others to observe teachers enjoying teaching and children enjoying learning. It is inspirational to be with teachers and children who go about the business of education with a serious attitude toward learning, while at the same time they enjoy the experience. The descriptive examples that follow are a synthesis of my study and observations in recent years in many different kinds of early childhood settings. The purpose of the examples is to share insights into what generates feelings of joy and pleasure during the educational process. These vignettes have implications for those who wish to study this area further as they consider ways to guide school life and learning activities to bring joy to both teachers and children. It is to this end that the entire monograph is addressed.

A HAPPY BEGINNING

The beginning of each school day is the teacher's opportunity to build a good educational climate by providing expressions of joy and establishing a positive mood for learning. Children are reminded that they are welcome in "their" school, and that each day there will be events that will bring them joy. When teachers explain the day's activities each morning with language and attitude that generates positive suspense and anticipation, a stage of opportunity is set for generating feelings of joy throughout the day. Welcomes and greetings joyfully expressed will beget other joyful welcomes and greetings. Demonstrating how to give happy greetings to others will help children develop a mind set for greeting others, and children will soon learn that they, too, can give joy to others through greetings. Having children greet all other members of their group daily, using a variety of happy greetings, could help them to establish life patterns that will become more and more refined and effectual as they become older.

MY SCHOOL, OUR SCHOOL

Children have a special need to know that they share in the ownership and in the success of their school, an ownership that includes their rights to quality learning opportunities, and the assurance that they each have a uniqueness that the school will serve. The inner feelings issuing from such understanding of personal worth can both stimulate a response of joy and become the driving force that encourages full participation in school life. As children develop an awareness that others are experiencing joy in learning in school, that "my" school will help me to enjoy learning, and that "my" school will prepare me to enjoy learning as I grow older (get bigger), attitudes can be formed that will have a positive effect on the development of long-range values toward schooling.

There are some special ways children can become involved in decision making in "their school." Let the children help to decide what they would like their parents to see when they visit the school on "parent's night." If a decision is made to show some of the children's work, let them help to decide what to show and how to display it. If a piece of playground equipment is soon to be purchased for the school, involve the children in looking at a catalog showing the equipment and discuss with them which item might be better than another one. The goal is to involve children in the process of recommending and making decisions that have something to do with the operation of their school. Look for simple ways to help them individually to feel a sense of ownership of their school.

QUALITY EXPERIENCE

The quality of each activity and experience in the child's school day will have much to do with generating feelings of joy. Even the youngest mind is capable of recognizing quality experience. The teacher who is well-organized and able to guide children through logical sequences of interesting and challenging activities will give children a sense of joy because what they did worked. Attractively prepared learning materials experienced in a classroom embellished with a continual flow of fresh visual and age-appropriate displays of materials related to what they are learning will also be a source of joy. Order; dependable routines; opportunities for each child to participate in the affairs of the class and the school; physical settings organized so that children know which space is theirs and which spaces are to be shared; a knowledge of where things are located and where they are to be stored after use; a knowledge of procedures that relate to their sense of well-being in regard to safety, illness, toilet emergencies, and other such matters, all relate directly to the recognition of quality—quality that will bring gladness, delight, and pleasure. Building positive attitudes toward good quality in all aspects of a child's school day could contribute to learning becoming a lifelong source of joy. Children are entitled to the best quality of educational experience that we are able to provide.

TEACHABLE MOMENTS

There are often unexpected occasions in school life that create tension and present periods of unpleasantness, undoing a state of enjoyment established earlier. Teachers are encouraged to view such occasions as teachable moments, and to discuss with the children what has happened, to talk things through with them to learn what caused the unpleasantness and how they might work together to restore the level of pleasantness that existed earlier. A goal is to guide children to recognize how human behavior, unusual weather, the failure of utilities and motors, and other such things can result in unpleasant situations in life. Such occasions also can be very fearful for young children because feelings of uncertainty are generated by not understanding or knowing the sources or causes of what has happened. Children need to understand from an early age how events, circumstances, and a variety of unexpected disruptions can result in joyless periods of time. They especially need to learn about things that cause unpleasantness and the ways human behavior and other occurrences can be adjusted to reverse the situation.

There are also pleasant, planned, and unplanned occasions that offer valuable teachable moments. These might be a surprise visitor to the classroom, a surprise party for a classmate, news about a special excursion to a favorite place, something one class is going to do for another class, and so on. When a surprise or planned event or happening occurs or is announced that brings joy to students, discuss with them what it was that caused them to suddenly feel joyful. It is as important for children to become sensitive to what causes joy as it is for them to know what causes the lack of joy. Giving attention to such matters will prepare children to become more conscious of things that can contribute to joy, eventually creating a mind-set for seeking it out.

MY RIGHTS, YOUR RIGHTS, OUR RIGHTS

The social development of children at an early age—particularly with respect to recognizing the rights of other children—is a key to enjoyment in schooling. As children individually learn to recognize that other children also have a specialness, and that they, too, share in the ownership of the school, a friendly and pleasurable environment can be established. Children who learn to take personal pride in the successes of other children, who learn to be sympathetic to the needs of others, who learn the value both of having a friend and of being a friend, have another source of gladness, delight, and pleasure that will contribute to success in learning.

Children need occasions to discuss as a group how they can show friendship to others. Help them focus on what being a friend means, how they can do friendly things for someone they do not know, how friends can help each other in a time of need, and how one should always be concerned about the welfare of another friend. The purpose should be to impress upon children the need to respect the rights of all other children as a means of developing friendships.

MOODS FROM HOME, MOODS AT SCHOOL

Varied events and activities in the home and the school will often cause young children to experience different moods for periods of time. Joy, of course, is not a feeling that children will experience all day every day. Lack of sleep, problems with siblings, a lost favorite toy, physical illness, severe verbal abuse by adults, and other kinds of experiences will generate feelings different from joy. It is important for educators of young children to recognize that they cannot resolve all of the difficult situations in a child's life, or provide the same degree of attention and nurturing for each child that loving and caring parents can provide. It is essential, however, that teachers help children to find pleasure in their school lives, and to ensure that they will derive joy from learning activities. Theoretically, the more children experience joy in school, the greater the likelihood that they will develop an awareness of how joy can become a part of their nonschool lives, and they will seek ways to experience it through their own initiative. Favorable dispositions developed in one area of life often find ways to be developed in other areas.

IMPROVING CONDITIONS

Joy is also a state of happiness derived from the improvement of conditions that, from time to time, negatively affect all other relationships. The resolution of children's problems that occur in their relationships with others is therefore very important to their finding joy in the school experience. For some children, school may be the only place where they can have even a hope of experiencing joy because of the unhappy conditions that exist in the home. The restoration of friendships, the comfort derived from conflicts in school that have been resolved, and the ongoing reassurance that school is a place where each child has rights, and that joy can be found by all is important to successful learning. And oftentimes such enjoyable conditions in the school will even take the edge off negative nonschool conditions that children experience. Experiencing happy outcomes of problem situations in a child's school life is a key to continued success, and teachers need to work constantly at contributing to the resolution of such problems.

POSITIVE OUTCOMES

Another source of joy in learning are the positive outcomes children experience in learning activities. Good results from children's efforts to learn will generate feelings of pleasure and satisfaction. Therefore, a healthy proportion of learning activities for young children should be planned to ensure success. Positive outcomes help to enlarge the personal sense of well-being, and it is only through experiencing success that children can develop an appetite for other successes. Then, as they reach higher levels of maturity, children begin to understand how personal effort can lead to success, and success can lead to joy. Educational encounters for young children need to be designed to introduce children to having successful outcomes and results so that they will learn how joy can be a part of the reward when they try.

SCHOOL ENVIRONMENTS

School and classroom environments have much to do with enjoyment in learning. Children need the reassurance that the classroom environment is planned for them, and that sometimes it is even adjusted to accommodate their individual and collective needs. The physical environment should always be planned to stimulate learning and to extend the relationship with what is to be learned. Often, displays and decorative materials attached to walls are provided as space fillers, and they have been known to remain in their established strongholds for great lengths of time. *Freshness* is an absolute must in educating young children to maintain an ongoing open attitude toward newness—new and catchy materials, new thought stimulators, new creative suggestions, new suspense builders, new challenges, and new explorations. Exciting learning environments are absolutely essential in childhood education. But a basic concern is that learning environments should be planned to guide children in developing higher level thinking skills in pleasurable, nonthreatening, and challenging ways.

VARIETY OF OBJECTS AND EVENTS

Children should have many objects in their lives from which they can derive joy. Toys, tools, household articles, and other such objects that they can manipulate and use in play from time to time, will be a source of delight for children. Occasions for exploration, manipulation, and free play with such objects is a vital part of childhood education programs. Excursions, resource persons, visiting performing groups, school plays and programs, special thematic events, and a host of other kinds of activities are vital to school life. It is essential to have summary discussions with children about what they learned from such experiences; in addition, it is important to learn whether they found pleasure in what they experienced, and what it was about the experience that resulted in their enjoyment. Children will profit from developing an expanding awareness of why they enjoy some things and not others. It is believed that regularly focusing on the value of joy in life, and the factors that contribute to its value, will develop a consciousness that will leave lifelong imprints of the value of joy.

DRESS, EMOTIONAL SET, SPEECH, VOCABULARY

Early childhood programs should provide children with enjoyable educational experiences, but they should also lay the *foundation* for becoming a productive, successful adult who will live in a complex society. Given this belief, teachers need to provide good models for children in appearance, temperament, speech, and the vocabulary they use. Norman Cousins, in an article titled "The Decline of Neatness" (11), establishes what he believes are direct relationships between the way people dress, their emotional set, their speech, and the vocabulary they use. His article discusses the impact of television, the kinds of programs children are exposed to today, and the power they have to desensitize children regarding respect for human life.

The early childhood teacher (and hopefully, teachers at higher levels) can help to reduce the power of television by modeling other kinds of behavior—behavior that demonstrates sensitivity, care, and concern for human life. Having a first-hand experience with affectionate and loving teacher models will have a far greater impact on young minds than the television programs they might see; hence, the need for teachers to lay a foundation for showing respect for others, and the recognition that each child in the group has a special worth. Norman Cousins's article presents many important points that need to be considered by educators at all levels, and a careful reading will be of special benefit to all.

AFFECTION AND TOUCH

It is likely that most young children will have had several years of intimacy with parents and others prior to their participation in organized schooling. These years are usually filled with hugs, kisses, cuddling, and other ways of showing affection. Children enjoy receiving affection from others, as do most people of any age. And children who have developed a sense of security from the affection they received in their earlier days need to be shown a level of affection by teachers. This can be achieved in many different ways.

Special, kind words spoken to individual children during brief one-to-one encounters during the school day will be of great value to a child. And speaking the words with a hand placed on the shoulder, an arm around the back, a brief stroking of the child's hair, or a gentle patting on the head or back adds a valuable dimension to the experience. It is very important that during this period of time when the news media are reporting so many cases of child molestation in early childhood settings that the value of touch in a child's life is not totally abandoned. Even holding a child's hand during an activity is a form of touch that will have special meaning.

Insightful early childhood teachers will find reasonable ways to show affection to children without compromising their professionalism. The feelings of belonging, personal worth, and security that expressions of affection can generate need to be addressed and provided in some form in organized school life. The transition years from home to school and the necessity to adjust to becoming one of many students in a group should be gradual and marked with a level of affection. A show of affection by teachers will make a significant difference in children's inclination toward learning and the level of joy they will experience in organized schooling.

PRAISE LANGUAGE

Expressions of praise by teachers for efforts, progress, and behavior are a prime source of joy in the life of a child. Even older people find joy in expressions of appreciation for things that they have done well. Although the rewards of such expressions are

71

often short-lived, they do provide incentives for young children and suggest that recognition will be given for their future cooperative effort and hard work.

Some early childhood teachers use praise language throughout the school day—everything children do is praised, and praised again. This practice lessens the value of praise over a period of time and praise becomes commonplace and has little meaning for a child. It is important to find something that each child can be praised for; praise will have much greater meaning when it is reserved for those special occasions when it is warranted. Even children know when they have not done something well or that their cooperation level was not what it should have been.

There is also great value in praising individual children privately rather than before the entire group. Some children have been known to benefit more from private expressions of praise. But at other times, praise given before the entire group might be more appropriate. The *way* praise is expressed to children is very important. Matter-of-fact expressions without eye contact and without a child feeling that *this is being said about ME* will not be accepted as true praise. It is interesting to note that even though children are not inclined to give verbal opposition, they do have a sense for recognizing "phony" expressions. Honesty is important to young children for they will usually learn to model that which they have experienced repeatedly over a period of time.

RUSH-HOUR TEACHING

A majority of workers in our country—even teachers of young children—live their lives under rush-hour conditions. This mode of thinking and living impacts teachers in many different ways. The rush at home to prepare to leave in the morning, the rush to get to school, the rush to meet educational expectations in teaching, the rush to get home, the rush to complete a host of activities before sleeping—the story repeats itself day after day.

Young children generally only "go along for the ride" during the rush-hour escapades of their parents. They do not respond to the rush-hour mentality as more mature people do, nor do they adapt their ways of learning in a way that reflects a need to rush. There is a very important message teachers need to receive from children's seemingly impervious response to the rush-hour tactics of adults.

Early childhood teachers need to "down shift" (as with vehicles to make them go slower) and adapt to the children's pace(s) in the pursuit of meeting educational goals and objectives. Many teachers, often without realizing it, will set impossible expectations for children and impose unrealistic time limitations for their activities. There always will be some children who are capable of responding positively and adapting to time constraints. But there also will be many more children who ignore stress-filled, time-impossible practices because they are incapable of performing in a rushed mode. Even young children of the same age are often dramatically different in regard to concepts of time and work schedules. Helping them develop such abilities requires patience and usually a much longer time period than teachers want to provide. Teachers are encouraged to help children to *gradually* become sensitized to do schoolwork within realistic time frames. The imposition of time constraints on children who are incapable of meeting the expectations results in joyless school experiences. The adaptation of methods, materials, expectations, and rush-hour ideas to the pace(s) of young children is the only way to ensure that each child will find joy in learning.

COURTESY LANGUAGE

Courtesy language (*excuse me, pardon me, I'm sorry, I made a mistake*) has been described as a lost art. Many things that happen during a young child's school life generate unhappy feelings, but they could be tempered by the use of courtesy language. A child is accidentally bumped; a child is unintentionally poked, scratched, or hit; a child spills something on items belonging to another child; something belonging to one child is inadvertently taken and used by another child—the list goes on. Expressions of regret for what has happened can help to resolve joyless feelings.

Children learn courtesy language from observing others and understanding the situations that caused them to use it. Therefore, teachers should find opportunities to model courtesy language frequently during each day's activities. When children unintentionally do things that cause discomfort or bad feelings among others, and they do not know what to say, the teacher should model solutions. Courtesy language used appropriately can contribute much to the resolution of difficulties between children and restore a previously experienced level of joy. When early childhood education is viewed as a time for laying the foundation for a successful and productive adult life, the value of courtesy language becomes apparent.

LEARNING HOW TO LEARN

It was stated in the philosophy section that the early years are a time for children to learn how to learn and to build an inner excitement for continued learning and greater explorations. When approached in the right way, children *always* enjoy learning new information and developing new skills related to what they have learned. Teachers need to follow-up children's successful learning experiences by helping them to understand *how* they learned—how they went about it, the steps involved, the way one step might have led to another, the kinds of things they had to think about, how they knew they were on the right track, surprises that occurred along the way and if their success caused them to enjoy learning. The purpose is to help them establish in their minds relationships between successful learning and enjoyable educational experience. Repeated successful learning experiences will gradually build a disposition toward future learning, and if approached from the point of view of the enjoyment that it will bring, it is possible that good attitudes toward schooling and learning will be formed.

It is recommended that on special days teachers prepare children to bring something from home (toy, game, simple object of some kind) that they will teach another child to use. The children could be paired so that the item brought from home will be unfamiliar to one child in each pair. After a child has taught another child how to use or play with the item, the learner should describe what was told to him/her by the "teacher" and how he/she learned to use or play with it. The value of such activities lies in understanding *how* they learned. A similar approach is used by insightful teachers. They have children who have learned to become "teachers" for those who have not yet learned. Peer teaching/tutoring oftentimes can add an enjoyable dimension to children's learning experience and aid the learning process in a direct way.

HAPPY FACES

I have observed and colleagues have validated that on occasions following visitations to classes for young children, a conclusion was drawn that "the teacher would benefit greatly from a smile transplant." Some teacher faces have a gloomy look because of heredity, others are the result of to a lack of joyful feelings about different aspects of life. Unfortunately, gloomy teacher faces beget gloomy learner faces. It is amazing, however, that some teachers who have gloomy facial expressions as a result of heredity can diminish the impact on children by the soft, thoughtful words they speak and the nurturing actions they consistently demonstrate. As in all human behavior, a seemingly negative characteristic can often be diluted by a positive quality.

Gloomy teacher faces caused by the lack of joyful feelings are a kind of cancer in early childhood education. Either a change in attitude or a change in profession would be the best solution for young children who need the special care and nurturing that only a joyful and sensitive teacher can provide. If feelings of joy and happiness can be fostered in the early years, there is a much greater likelihood that children will find learning and schooling to be enjoyable in future years.

A HAPPY ENDING

The closing of a school day provides an excellent opportunity for guiding children to recall and reflect on the activities of the day. What did we do today? What important things did we learn? What things were not finished that we need to work on some more? What activities did you think were most enjoyable? Why were they enjoyable? What activities would you like to do again? Helping children respond to questions such as these focuses attention on what learning is about and their personal involvement in school life. Children's names could be called in relation to the kinds of activities in which they were involved; this personalizes the occasion and builds a sense of "our" school day.

The closing could also be used to build interest and anticipation for the events of the next school day. New activities and their purposes could be briefly described in the form of new adventures and explorations. Building excitement in children about learning and promoting positive attitudes toward future learning will have a lot to do with developing a positive disposition toward it. Arousing the curiosity of young children about things they might learn or do is a natural way to stimulate interest in new educational adventures.

Chapter 9

CODA

Young children are the delight of parents and people of all ages in all cultures of the world. There is something so unique and charming about them that people everywhere—when coming into the presence of young children—smile and have an immediate feeling of affection and the desire to touch and communicate with them in some way. Perhaps it is their innocence and bias-free lives that signal to the world that people should have thoughts as pure as those of young children. Their child qualities warm and charm us and stimulate feelings of joy within us. These same kinds of qualities often find their way into the lives of early childhood teachers. A general openness about life, an adventurous spirit, a loving and caring nature, a sense of honesty and fair play, a feeling of respect for other people and the things that belong to others, a joyful attitude toward life, a spirit of cooperativeness, an excitement about learning and developing new skills, and many other such qualities typify many early childhood teachers throughout the world today. Good educational programs for young children directed by teachers with such qualities are the *hope* for improving upper elementary and secondary education in our country.

A restructuring of schools to teach human values in tandem with the traditional subjects could become a new beginning for improving life in our country. Of course, this is not a new idea. Some secondary schools have courses in which human values are taught, but such values should be taught as a common staple in all courses at all levels. A majority of high school students might become intellectual giants by the time of graduation, but what difference will that make if they do not have the childlike values and qualities that will help them to live successfully with themselves and with others? It just may be possible that early childhood educators should be consulted to assist in planning education for the future at the secondary level. After all, on how many occasions have secondary- and college-level teachers influenced the design of early childhood educational programs?

REFERENCES

1. Gaylin, W. *Feelings: Listen to Your Feelings and Understand Them.* New York: Ballantine Books, 1979, p. 200.
2. Ibid., pp. 202–208.
3. Burton, L. H., and Kuroda, K. *Arts Play: Creative Activities in Art, Music, Dance, and Drama for Young Children.* Menlo Park, Calif: Addison-Wesley, 1981.
4. National Association for the Education of Young Children. "Position Statement on Developmentally Appropriate Practice in Programs for 4- and 5-Year-Olds." *Young Children,* September 1986. Or see Bredekamp, S., ed. *Developmentally Appropriate Practice in Early Childhood Programs Serving Children from Birth Through Age 8.* Washington, D.C.: National Association for the Education of Young Children, 1987.
5. Montessori, M. *Childhood Education.* New York: New American Library, 1975.
6. Word W. *Playmaking with Children.* New York: Appleton-Century Crofts, 1957.
7. Bruner, J. *The Process of Education.* Cambridge: Harvard University Press, 1962.
8. Association for Supervision and Curriculum Development. *Interdisciplinary Curriculum: Design and Implementation.* Alexandria, Va.: the Association, 1989.
9. Taylor, Ann Baldwin, Director, Children's School. Carnegie-Mellon University, Pittsburgh, Pa. Verbal communication to author, 1990.
10. Levinger, L., and Adler, J. "How Children Learn." *Good Housekeeping* (Child Care '90 issue, September 1990).
11. Cousins, N. "The Decline of Neatness." *Time* (April, 1990).